Christmas Treat Recipes

Hannie P. Scott

CONTENTS

Download My FREE Gift!

Breakfast, Lunch, Dinner, Soups, Salads, Desserts and More!

Please visit: www.HanniepScott.com/freegift

i

Abbreviations

oz = ounce
fl oz = fluid ounce
tsp = teaspoon
tbsp = tablespoon
ml = milliliter
c = cup
pt = pint
qt = quart
gal = gallon
L = liter

Conversions

1/2 fl oz = 3 tsp = 1 tbsp = 15 ml
1 fl oz = 2 tbsp = 1/8 c = 30 ml
2 fl oz = 4 tbsp = 1/4 c = 60 ml
4 fl oz = 8 tbsp = 1/2 c = 118 ml
8 fl oz = 16 tbsp = 1 c = 236 ml
16 fl oz = 1 pt = 1/2 qt = 2 c = 473 ml
128 fl oz = 8 pt = 4 qt = 1 gal = 3.78 L

Candies

Peanut Butter Fudge

Makes 50 pieces of fudge

What you need:

- 3/4 cup of butter
- 1 5-oz can of evaporated milk
- 3 cups sugar
- 1 1/2 cups peanut butter
- 1 7-oz jar marshmallow cream
- 1 tsp vanilla extract

What to do:

1. Spray a 9x13-inch baking dish with cooking spray.
2. In a medium saucepan over medium heat, stir together the butter, evaporated milk, and sugar. Cook until the mixture reaches a boil and boil for 5 minutes then remove from heat.
3. Stir in the peanut butter, marshmallow cream, and vanilla until thoroughly mixed.
4. Pour the mixture into the prepared baking dish and spread evenly with a spatula.
5. Cool and refrigerate for several hours.
6. Cut into 1-inch squares and store in an air tight container.

Gingerbread Cheesecake Bites

Servings: 12

What you need:

- · 1 tbsp gingerbread coffee creamer
- · 8 oz cream cheese, at room temperature
- · 2 tbsp powdered sugar
- · 1 cup cool whip
- · 1/2 cup gingersnap crumbs

What to do:

1. Using an electric mixer, mix the creamer, cream cheese, and powdered sugar until smooth and creamy.
2. Mix in the cool whip.
3. Cover and place in freezer for an hour.
4. Remove from freezer and roll into 1-inch balls.
5. Roll in gingersnap crumbs.
6. Lay the covered balls on a baking sheet lined with parchment paper and freezer for 2 hours before serving.

Rolo Pretzel Sandwiches

Makes 25 sandwiches

What you need:

- 50 small square pretzels
- 25 Rolo's
- 8 oz white chocolate chips
- Green and red sprinkles

What to do:

1. Preheat your oven to 250 degrees F and line a baking sheet with parchment paper.
2. Place 25 pretzels onto the parchment paper.
3. Place a Rolo onto each pretzel.
4. Place the baking sheet in the oven and bake for 3-4 minutes or until the Rolos have softened but not melted.
5. Remove the baking sheet from the oven and place a square pretzel on top of each Rolo and gently press down. You want it to be sandwiched but you don't want the caramel to squish out.
6. Let them cool completely.
7. After they're cooled, melt the white chocolate.
8. Dip each Rolo pretzel sandwich into the white chocolate and place back onto the baking sheet to dry.
9. Apply the red and green sprinkles immediately after placing each sandwich back on the baking sheet.

Hay Stacks

Makes 2 dozen

What you need:

- 1 cup butterscotch chips
- 1/2 cup peanut butter
- 1/2 cup peanuts
- 2 cups chow mein noodles

What to do:

1. Microwave the butterscotch chips and the peanut butter in a large microwave safe bowl for 2-3 minutes, stirring every 30 seconds.
2. Remove the bowl from the microwave and stir in the peanuts and the chow mein noodles.
3. Spoon dollops of the mixture onto wax paper or parchment paper. Let sit for 2-3 hours or until completely cooled and hardened.
4. Serve immediately or store in an airtight container.

Christmas Marshmallow Pops

Makes about 3 dozen*

What you need:

- 1 bag large marshmallows
- 1 large bag mini candy canes
- 1 large block of chocolate
- Crushed candy canes

What to do:

1. Stick a mini candy cane into each large marshmallow.
2. Melt the chocolate in the microwave or over a double boiler.
3. Dip each marshmallow into the chocolate.
4. Roll each chocolate dipped marshmallow in the crushed candy canes.
5. Place on wax paper to dry.

*You can easily adjust this recipe to make whatever amount of servings you want!

Three Ingredient Fudge

Servings: 8

What you need:

- 1 cup dark chocolate chips
- 1 cup of coconut milk
- 1/4 cup of honey

What to do:

1. Mix all of the ingredients together in a microwave safe bowl and microwave for 30 seconds at a time until completely melted. Stir after every 30 second interval.
2. Stir until the mixture is smooth.
3. Pour the fudge mixture into a greased 9x9 baking dish.
4. Cover the fudge with plastic wrap and refrigerate for at least 3 hours before serving.

Christmas Peppermint Bark

Servings: 10-12

What you need:

- 12 oz chocolate chips
- 12-oz white chocolate chips
- 1 tsp peppermint extract
- 1/2 cup crushed peppermints

What to do:

1. Line a baking sheet with parchment paper and spray with non-stick spray.
2. Place the semi-sweet chocolate chips in a microwave safe bowl for 2 minutes, stirring every 30 seconds.
3. Pour the melted chocolate onto the prepared pan and spread into an even layer. Let cool.
4. Repeat step 2 with the white chocolate chips then stir in the peppermint extract.
5. Spread this mixture onto the cooled chocolate layer on the baking sheet.
6. Sprinkle the crushed peppermints onto the white chocolate layer and gently press the pieces in with a spatula.
7. Let cool then break into pieces before serving.

Christmas Sugar Cookie Truffles

Makes 18 Truffles

What you need:

- 12 sugar cookies
- 3 tbsp cream cheese, at room temperature
- 2 cups white chocolate chips
- Christmas sprinkles

What to do:

1. Place the sugar cookies in a food processor and pulse until fine crumbs form. Add cream cheese and process again until mixed.
2. Shape the mixture into 1-inch balls and place them on a baking sheet lined with parchment paper or a baking mat.
3. Place the baking sheet in the freezer for 15 minutes.
4. Melt the white chocolate chips in a microwave safe bowl for 30 seconds at a time in the microwave until melted. Stir after every 30 second interval.
5. Remove the cookie balls from the freezer and using two forks, dip each one into white chocolate, covering it completely. Return the balls to the baking sheet and immediately top with sprinkles before the white chocolate dries.
6. Store in an airtight container in the refrigerator.

Cinnamon Sugar Pecans

Servings: 10

What you need:

- 1 egg white
- 2 tsp water
- 2 tsp vanilla extract
- 1 lb pecan halves
- 1 cup sugar
- 1 tbsp ground cinnamon
- 1/2 tsp salt

What to do:

1. Preheat your oven to 250 degrees F.
2. Spray a baking sheet with cooking spray.
3. In a large Ziploc bag, mix together the cinnamon, sugar, and salt.
4. Whisk the egg white, water, and vanilla in a large bowl until frothy.
5. Add the pecans to the large bowl and stir to coat each pecan in egg white mixture.
6. Pour the coated pecans into the Ziploc bag, seal, and shake to fully coat the pecans in the cinnamon and sugar mixture.
7. Spread evenly onto the prepared baking sheet.
8. Bake for 1 hour, stirring every 15-20 minutes.

Divinity

Servings: 8

What you need:

- 2 cups sugar
- 1/2 cup white corn syrup
- 1/2 cup water
- 2 egg whites
- Pinch of salt
- 1 tsp pure vanilla
- 1 cup chopped pecans

What to do:

1. Heat the sugar, corn syrup, and water over medium heat in a large saucepan.
2. Using a candy thermometer, heat the mixture to 250 degrees F.
3. While the sugar mixture is cooking, whip the egg whites and salt until stiff peaks form.
4. When the sugar mixture has reached 250 degrees F, remove it from the heat and slowly pour it into the beaten egg whites, whipping together on high with an electric mixer.
5. Add the vanilla and continue mixing on high until it holds its shape, about 5 minutes.
6. Stir in the chopped pecans.
7. Working quickly, use two spoons to drop scoops of the mixture onto a baking sheet lined with parchment paper.

8. Allow the divinity to harden for several hours or overnight. Store in an airtight container.

Pecan Turtle Clusters

Makes about 20 clusters

What you need:

- 50-60 pecan halves
- 20 soft caramels
- 7 oz sweetened condensed milk
- 2 tbsp butter
- 12 oz chocolate chips
- Sea salt, optional

What to do:

1. Toast the pecans on a baking sheet at 300 degrees F for about 6 minutes then remove from the oven and let cool.
2. Unwrap the caramels and place them in a microwave safe bowl with the condensed milk and butter. Microwave for 30 seconds at a time until melted. Stir between every 30 second interval.
3. Line 2 baking sheets with parchment paper.
4. Arrange the pecans in small clusters of about 3 pecans.
5. Spoon a spoonful of caramel onto each cluster.
6. Melt the chocolate chips by the same method as you melted the caramels.
7. Spoon a spoonful of chocolate on top of the caramel.
8. Add a sprinkle of sea salt to each, if desired.
9. Refrigerate for a couple hours until set then store in an airtight container.

Martha Washingtons

Makes about 6 dozen

What you need:

- 14-oz sweetened coconut flakes
- 14-oz can of sweetened condensed milk
- 2 cups of powdered sugar
- 1 cup butter, melted
- 1 1/2 cups finely chopped pecans
- 12-oz chocolate chips
- 1 tbsp coconut oil

What to do:

1. In a mixing bowl with a paddle attachment, mix together the coconut, sweetened condensed milk, powdered sugar, melted butter, and pecans until combined well.
2. Cover and refrigerate for several hours.
3. After refrigerating, roll the mixture into 1-inch (or a little smaller) balls and lay out on a baking sheet lined with parchment paper (you will probably need more than 1).
4. Place the baking sheets and balls in the refrigerator.
5. Melt the chocolate chips and coconut oil in a microwave safe bowl in the microwave for 30 seconds at a time until melted, stirring after every 30 second interval.
6. Quickly dip balls one at a time into the chocolate using a toothpick or fork then lay back on the parchment paper.

7. Refrigerate for a couple hours until set then store in an airtight container in the refrigerator.

Buckeyes

Aka peanut butter balls

Makes about 3 dozen balls

What you need:

- 12 oz natural peanut butter
- 1 stick butter, at room temperature
- 1 tsp vanilla
- 1 lb powdered sugar
- 16 oz chocolate chips

What to do:

1. In a mixing bowl with a mixing, beat the peanut butter and butter until smooth. Mix in the vanilla.
2. At low speed, gradually add in the powdered sugar and beat until smooth.
3. Roll into 1-inch balls and place on a baking sheet lined with parchment paper. Place in freezer for 1 hour.
4. Melt the chocolate in the microwave 30 seconds at a time until fully melted. Stir after every 30 second interval.
5. Dip the chilled peanut butter balls 3/4 of the way into the melted chocolate and place back on the parchment paper covered baking sheet to dry.
6. Store in an airtight container in the refrigerator.

Hot Chocolate Fudge

Servings: 10

What you need:

- 2 cups chocolate chips
- 14 oz sweetened condensed milk
- 1 cup white chocolate chips
- 1 1/2 cups mini marshmallows

What to do:

1. Line a 9x9-inch baking dish with parchment paper and spray with cooking spray.
2. In a microwave safe bowl, stir together the white chocolate chips and 3 tbsp of the sweetened condensed milk. Set aside.
3. In another bowl, combine the chocolate chips and the remaining sweetened condensed milk. Microwave 30 seconds at a time until completely melted. Stir between each interval.
4. Pour the melted chocolate into the prepared baking dish and spread out.
5. Microwave the white chocolate 30 seconds at a time until completely melted. Stir between each interval.
6. Pour the melted white chocolate over the chocolate in the dish.
7. Top with mini marshmallows and gently press down.
8. Refrigerate for several hours.
9. Remove from pan and cut into squares.

White Chocolate Caramel Pecan Fudge

Makes about 3 dozen

What you need:

· 3 cups white chocolate chips
· 14-oz sweetened condensed milk
· 4 tbsp butter
· 1/2 tsp vanilla extract
· 1 cup chopped pecans
· 1/2 cup caramel sauce

What to do:

1. Line a 9x13-inch baking dish with parchment paper.
2. Place the white chocolate chips, milk, and butter in a microwave safe bowl and microwave 30 seconds at a time until melted completely. Stir after every 30 second interval.
3. Stir in the vanilla extract and pecans and mix well.
4. Pour the mixture onto the baking dish and spread out evenly.
5. Drizzle with caramel sauce and lightly swirl the sauce into the fudge.
6. Chill in the refrigerator for several hours or until ready to serve.
7. Cut into 1-inch squares.

Ice Cube Tray Chocolates

Servings: 16

What you need:

- 2 1/2 cups milk chocolate chips
- 2 tbsp coconut oil
- Cooking spray
- Ice cube tray
- Various fillings: chunky peanut butter, soft caramel chews, chopped peanuts, marshmallows

What to do:

1. Place the chocolate chips and coconut oil in a microwave safe bowl and microwave 30 seconds at a time until completely melted, stirring after each 30 second interval.
2. Spray the ice cube with cooking spray, making sure the whole cube section is covered with spray.
3. Fill each cube with chocolate about 1/3 of the way up.
4. Tilt the tray to make the chocolate coat the sides of the tray.
5. Freeze for 2 minutes.
6. Tilt the tray again to make the chocolate go up the sides.
7. Place fillings of choice into the trays. Make sure that the filling stays in the middle and doesn't touch the sides.
8. Cover with remaining chocolate to the top.
9. Freeze for an hour until the chocolate hardens then remove from the freezer and remove the chocolates from the tray.

Peanut Brittle

Servings: 8

What you need:

· 1 cup sugar
· 1/2 cup corn syrup
· 1 cup peanuts
· 1 tsp butter
· 1 tsp vanilla extract
· 1 tsp baking soda

What to do:

1. Line a baking sheet with parchment paper and spray with non-stick spray.
2. In a 2 quart glass bowl, combine the sugar and corn syrup. Microwave on high for 4 minutes.
3. Stir in the peanuts and microwave for another 3 and a half minutes.
4. Stir in butter and vanilla and microwave for another minute and a half.
5. Stir in the baking soda and mix well.
6. Pour the mixture onto the prepared baking sheet and spread it out in a thin layer.
7. Let it cool completely then break into pieces before serving.

Christmas Muddy Buddies

Servings: 16

What you need:

· 14 cups Chex cereal
· 18 oz red and green M&M's
· 12 oz semi-sweet chocolate chips
· 1/2 cup butter
· 1 cup peanut butter
· 1 tsp vanilla extract
· 4-5 cups powdered sugar

What to do:

1. In a microwave safe bowl, melt the peanut butter and butter at 30 second intervals until butter is melted completely.
2. Add the chocolate and stir until they are melted, microwave at 30 second intervals if necessary.
3. Pour half of the Chex cereal into a very large bowl.
4. Drizzle half of the chocolate/peanut butter mixture over the cereal and mix with a spoon.
5. Pour 1 cup of powdered sugar into a gallon zip lock bag and add half of the covered cereal mix. Close the bag and shake until the cereal is coated.
6. Repeat step 5 until all of the coated cereal is covered in powdered sugar.
7. Repeat steps 3-6 until all cereal is covered in powdered sugar.

8. Place all of the cereal in a large container and toss in the M&M's.

Cookies

Christmas Shortbread Squares

Servings: about 30

What you need:

- 1 cup butter, cold and diced into 1 tbsp pieces
- 2/3 cup sugar
- 1/2 tsp almond extract
- 2 1/4 cups flour
- 2 1/2 tbsp Christmas sprinkles

What to do:

1. Spray a 9x13 inch baking dish with cooking spray. Cut a piece of parchment paper a little longer than the length of your baking dish and line the dish lengthwise. Spray the parchment paper. Cut another piece of parchment paper a little longer than the width of your baking dish and line the dish widthwise.
2. In the bowl of a stand mixer, cream together the butter and sugar until combined. Mix in the almond extract.
3. At low speed, slowly mix in the flour until it is combined well.
4. Fold in the sprinkles.
5. Press the dough into an even layer in the prepared pan.
6. Refrigerate for 30 minutes.
7. Preheat your oven to 350 degrees F.
8. Using the parchment paper, lift the dough out of the baking dish.
9. Cut into 1/2-inch squares.

10. Transfer about 1/3 of the cookie squares to a baking dish and bake for 8-10 minutes. Put the other squares in the fridge in the meantime.
11. Repeat the process with the remaining squares.
12. Cool completely then store in an airtight container until ready to serve.

3 Ingredient Shortbread Cookies

Makes about 3 dozen cookies

What you need:

· 2 cups butter, cold and cut into pieces
· 1 cup packed brown sugar
· 4 1/2 cups all-purpose flour, divided
· Optional: Christmas sprinkles

What to do:

1. In a mixing bowl, mix the butter and brown sugar with an electric mixer until creamy.
2. Add 3 1/2 cups of flour and mix until combined.
3. Sprinkle 1/2 cup of flour onto a large clean working surface.
4. Knead the dough by hand for 5 minutes, adding the remaining 1/2 cup of flour as needed to make the dough soft. Work in sprinkles too if you're using them.
5. Form a ball out of the dough and wrap it tightly in plastic wrap and refrigerate it for 30 minutes.
6. Preheat your oven to 325 degrees F and line 2 large baking sheets with parchment paper.
7. Roll the dough out onto a large working surface to about 1/2 inch thickness.
8. Cut into rectangles, triangles, or use cookie cutters to cut out shapes.
9. Place the cookies 1-inch apart on the prepared baking sheets.
10. Bake for 15-20 minutes or until the edges are golden brown.

11. Cool on a wire rack then serve or store in an airtight container.

Mint Kiss Cookies

Makes about 3 dozen

What you need:

- 1 ½ cups powdered sugar
- 1 1/4 cups butter, softened
- 1 tsp mint extract
- 1 tsp vanilla extract
- 1 large egg
- 3 cups all-purpose flour
- 1 tsp baking powder
- 1/2 tsp salt
- 1/2 cup finely chopped candy cane flavored Hershey's Kisses
- Granulated sugar
- Additional unwrapped Candy Cane Hershey's Kisses

What to do:

1. Preheat your oven to 350 degrees F and line a baking sheet with parchment paper.
2. In a mixing bowl, mix together the powdered sugar, butter, mint extract, vanilla extract, and egg with an electric mixer until creamy.
3. In a separate bowl, whisk together the flour, baking powder, and salt.
4. Slowly add the flour mixture to the sugar/butter mixture until combined.
5. Stir in the chopped Kisses with a spoon.

6. Shape the dough into 1-inch balls and roll in granulated sugar. Place the balls 1-inch apart on the prepared sheet.
7. Bake for 10-12 minutes or until slightly golden.
8. Let the cookies cool for 2-3 minutes on the baking sheet then press a Hershey's Kiss into each cookie.

Pumpkin Cheesecake Snickerdoodles

Makes 24 cookies

What you need:

· 3 3/4 cups all-purpose flour
· 1 1/2 tsp baking powder
· 1/2 tsp salt
· 1/2 tsp ground cinnamon
· 1/4 tsp ground nutmeg
· 1 cup butter, at room temperature
· 1 cup sugar
· 1/2 cup brown sugar
· 3/4 cup pumpkin puree
· 1 large egg
· 2 tsp vanilla extract

Filling:

· 8 oz cream cheese, at room temperature
· 1/4 cup sugar
· 2 tsp vanilla extract

Coating:

· 1/2 cup sugar
· 1 tsp cinnamon
· 1/2 tsp ground ginger
· Dash of allspice

What to do:

1. In a medium bowl, whisk together the flour, baking powder, salt, cinnamon, and nutmeg.
2. In a mixing bowl, beat together the butter and sugars with an electric mixer until fluffy.
3. Mix in the pumpkin puree and beat in the egg and vanilla.
4. Slowly add the dry ingredients to the wet ingredients and mix on low until just combined.
5. Cover and refrigerate the dough for an hour.
6. To make the filling, beat the cream cheese, sugar, and vanilla until smooth. Chill for an hour in the refrigerator.
7. Preheat your oven to 350 degrees F and line 2 large baking sheets with parchment paper or baking mats.
8. In a small bowl, stir together the sugar, cinnamon, ginger, and allspice. Set aside.
9. To form the cookies, take a tbsp of cookie batter and flatten it. Place a tsp of cream cheese mixture on the flattened cookie batter. Form another tbsp of cookie batter over the cream cheese mixture and pinch the edges to "seal" in the cream cheese. Roll the whole thing into a ball. Repeat with all of the dough and roll them in the cinnamon/sugar mixture.
10. Place them 1-2 inches apart on the baking sheets and press them down with a glass jar.
11. Bake the cookies for 10-15 minutes or until the tops begin to crack.
12. Remove from the oven and let cool before serving.

Snowball Cookies

Makes about 70 small cookies

What you need:

- 1 cup unsalted butter, at room temperature
- 5 tbsp granulated sugar
- 2 tsp vanilla extract
- 1/4 tsp salt
- 2 cups all-purpose flour
- 2 cups very finely chopped walnuts
- 1 1/2 cups powdered sugar

What to do:

1. Using an electric mixer, cream together the butter and sugar. Mix in the vanilla and salt.
2. Gradually add in the flour.
3. Stir in the finely chopped walnuts.
4. Divide the dough in half and refrigerate for an hour.
5. Preheat your oven to 350 degrees and line two baking sheets with parchment paper or baking mats.
6. Place powdered sugar in a small bowl and set aside.
7. Remove half of the dough from the refrigerator and roll into 1-inch balls. Place balls an inch apart on the prepared baking sheets.
8. Bake for 12 minutes or until the cookies are beginning to turn golden brown.

9. Remove and let cool for 2 minutes and gently roll them in powdered sugar while still warm. Place back on rack to cool completely. Roll them in sugar again after they've cooled completely.

10. Repeat steps 5-9 with second half of the dough. You could save the dough for another day. It will keep in your fridge for a week.

Rudolph Brownies

Servings: 8

What you need:

- 1/2 cup vegetable oil
- 1 cup sugar
- 1 tsp vanilla
- 2 large eggs
- 1/4 tsp baking powder
- 1/3 cup cocoa powder
- 1/4 tsp salt
- 1/2 cup all-purpose flour
- Edible candy eyes
- Chocolate icing
- Pretzels
- Round baking dish.

What to do:

1. Preheat your oven to 350 degrees F.
2. With an electric mixer, mix together the oil and sugar until mixed well.
3. Add in the eggs and vanilla and mix until just combined.
4. In a separate bowl, stir together the baking powder, cocoa powder, salt, and flour.
5. Stir the flour mixture into the sugar and egg mixture and combine.
6. Pour the batter into a greased round baking pan.
7. Bake for 20 minutes or until a toothpick inserted comes out clean.

8. Remove from the oven and let cool.
9. Cut the brownies like you would cut a pie or a pizza, into 8 triangles.
10. Break the pretzels in half and insert them into the wide end of the triangle to make reindeer horns.
11. Place a red M&M on the end of each triangle to be the nose.
12. Place edible eyes on each triangle. You can use a very small amount of icing to "glue" them down.

Desserts

Caramel Apple Cheesecake Dip

Servings: 12

What you need:

- 2 8-oz packages of cream cheese at room temperature
- 1/2 cup sugar
- 1/2 cup sour cream
- 1 tsp vanilla extract
- 1 can caramel apple pie filling
- 1/2 cup flour
- 3 tbsp butter, melted
- 1/4 cup brown sugar
- Graham Crackers

What to do:

1. Preheat your oven to 350 degrees F.
2. With an electric mixer, combine the cream cheese, sugar, sour cream, and vanilla until smooth and creamy.
3. Spread the mixture evenly into the bottom of a 10-inch pie plate.
4. Top with caramel apple pie filling.
5. In a small bowl, stir together the flour, melted butter, and brown sugar to make a streusel topping.
6. Sprinkle the topping over the apple pie filling.
7. Bake for 25 minutes.
8. Serve with graham crackers.

Mint Chocolate Dip

Servings: 6

What you need:

- 8-oz cream cheese, at room temperature
- 13 oz marshmallow cream
- 15 fudge mint cookies
- 1/4 cup mint M&Ms
- Cookies, for dipping

What to do:

1. Chop the cookies and M&Ms into small pieces.
2. In a mixing bowl with an electric mixer, whip the cream cheese until fluffy.
3. Mix in the marshmallow cream.
4. Stir in the chopped cookies and M&Ms.
5. Serve with cookies of choice.

Apple Cider Cobbler

Servings: 8

What you need:

· 2 20-oz cans of apple pie filling
· 2 tsp cinnamon
· 2 tsp nutmeg
· 1 11-oz bag of Kraft caramels
· 1 box of yellow cake mix
· 3/4 cup butter, melted

What to do:

1. Preheat your oven to 350 degrees F and grease a 9x13 inch baking dish.
2. In a bowl, stir together the apple pie filling, cinnamon, and nutmeg.
3. Pour the mixture into the baking dish and spread out evenly.
4. Unwrap each caramel and cut them in half. Top the apple mixture with the caramels.
5. Sprinkle the cake mix over the apples and caramel.
6. Slowly pour the melted butter over the cake mix. Try to "wet" as much of the cake mix with the butter as you can.
7. Bake for 45 minutes then serve with ice cream, if desired.

Gingerbread Pudding

Servings: 8

What you need:

- · 1 14-oz package of gingerbread mix
- · 1/2 cup milk
- · 1/2 cup raisins
- · 2 1/4 cups water
- · 1 cup packed brown sugar
- · 3/4 cup butter

What to do:

1. Coat your slow cooker with non-stick cooking spray.
2. In a medium bowl, combine the gingerbread mix and milk. Stir in the raisins. Spread the mixture into your slow cooker.
3. In a saucepan over medium-high heat, combine the water, brown sugar, and butter. Bring to a boil, reduce heat, and simmer for 5 minutes.
4. Pour the sugar mixture over the batter in the slow cooker.
5. Cook for 2 hours.
6. Turn off the slow cooker and let it sit for 1 hour without the lid.
7. Serve with vanilla ice cream, if desired.

Mini Egg Nog Cheesecakes

Servings: 9

What you need:

- 1 cup graham cracker crumbs
- 1/2 tsp nutmeg
- 2 tbsp butter, melted
- 12 oz cream cheese, softened
- 1/2 cup sugar
- 1/2 cup eggnog
- 1 tbsp flour
- 1 egg
- 1/4 tsp nutmeg
- 1/2 tsp vanilla

What to do:

1. Preheat your oven to 350 degrees F.
2. Line a muffin pan with 9 paper liners.
3. Combine the graham cracker crumbs, 1/2 tsp nutmeg, and melted butter.
4. Divide the graham cracker crumb mixture between the 9 paper liners and press down gently to flatten.
5. In a bowl with an electric mixer, combine the cream cheese and sugar together until fluffy.
6. Add in the egg, eggnog, flour, 1/4 tsp nutmeg, and vanilla. Mix well.
7. Evenly divide and spoon the mixture onto the 9 crusts.

8. Bake for 20 minutes or until centers are set then remove from the oven and allow them to cool completely in the pan.
9. Remove from the pan and refrigerate for 2 hours or more.

Pecan Pie Cheesecake

Servings: 8

What you need:

For the crust:

- 1 3/4 cups vanilla wafer crumbs
- 1/4 cup brown sugar
- 1/3 cup butter

For the Pecan Pie:

- 1 cup sugar
- 2/3 cup corn syrup
- 1/3 cup butter, melted
- 2 large eggs, beaten
- 1 1/2 cups chopped pecans
- 1 tsp vanilla extract

For the cheesecake:

- 24 oz cream cheese, at room temperature
- 1 1/4 cups light brown sugar
- 2 tbsp all-purpose flour
- 4 large eggs
- 2/3 cup heavy cream
- 1 tsp vanilla extract

For the topping:

- 1/4 cup butter, melted
- 1/2 cup brown sugar
- 1 tsp cinnamon
- 1/4 cup heavy whipping cream
- 1 cup toasted pecans, chopped

What to do:

For the crust:

1. Line the bottom of a 9-inch spring form pan with parchment paper and set aside.
2. Stir together the wafer crumbs and brown sugar. Stir in the melted butter and press the mixture evenly into the bottom and halfway up the spring form pan. Refrigerate.

For the Pecan Filling:

1. In a medium saucepan, stir the sugar, corn syrup, melted butter, eggs, pecans, and vanilla and bring the mixture to a boil over medium high heat. Stir constantly. Reduce heat and simmer while still stirring for 5 minutes or until thickened. Pour into the prepared crust and set aside.

For the Cheesecake:

1. Preheat your oven to 350 degrees F.
2. Beat the cream cheese until creamy and light. Add in the brown sugar and flour and beat until fluffy.

3. Add in the eggs, one at a time, beating lightly after each addition.
4. Stir in the heavy cream and vanilla until just mixed. Don't overmix.
5. Pour the cheesecake mixture over the pecan filling.
6. Place the spring form pan in the oven and reduce heat to 325 degrees F. Bake for 60 minutes or until a toothpick inserted comes out clean.
7. Turn off the oven and leave the oven door closed for an hour.
8. Run a knife around the edges of the cheesecake but don't remove it from the pan until it is all the way cooled.

For the Topping:

1. In a small saucepan, combine the butter and brown sugar and cook for 5 minutes.
2. Stir in the cinnamon, heavy whipping cream, and chopped pecans. Cool to room temperature.
3. Release the sides of the springform pan and spoon the topping over the cooled cheesecake.
4. Serve or store in refrigerator.

Gingerbread Cheesecake Dip

Servings: 8

What you need:

- 8-oz cream cheese, softened
- 1/4 cup brown sugar
- 1/4 cup powdered sugar
- 3 tbsp molasses
- 1 tsp ground ginger
- 1 tsp ground cinnamon
- 1/2 tsp nutmeg
- 4 oz Cool Whip
- Graham crackers for serving

What to do:

1. With an electric mixer, beat the cream cheese until smooth and fluffy.
2. Pour the brown sugar, powdered sugar and molasses into the cream cheese and beat until smooth.
3. Add in the ginger, cinnamon, and nutmeg and mix until smooth.
4. Stir in the Cool Whip.
5. Transfer to a serving dish and chill until time to serve.
6. Serve with graham crackers.

White Truffle Cake

Servings: 8

What you need:

- 3 eggs, at room temperature
- 1/3 cup sugar
- 1/3 cup flour
- 1 tsp vanilla extract
- 1 1/4 cups heavy cream
- 12 oz white chocolate chips
- 12 oz cream cheese

What to do:

1. Preheat your oven to 350 degrees F. Grease an 8" spring form pan.
2. Beat the eggs, vanilla, and sugar in a mixing bowl until white, foamy, and tripled in size.
3. Sift the flour and slowly add it to the egg mixture carefully.
4. Bake for 15-17 minutes until a knife inserted comes out clean.
5. Remove from oven and let cool.
6. In a medium saucepan over medium heat, bring the heavy cream to a simmer. Stir in the white chocolate chips and stir until melted. Let this mixture cool completely.
7. In a medium bowl with a mixer, whip the cream cheese until fluffy. Add the cream mixture to the cream cheese and whip until smooth. This is the truffle layer.

8. Pour the truffle layer on top of the cake layer in the spring form pan. Refrigerate for several hours until cold.
9. Run a knife along the edges then release it from the pan.

Gingerbread Bread Pudding

Servings: 8-10

What you need:

- 1 loaf of French bread, cut into 1" cubes
- 2 1/2 cups milk
- 5 eggs
- 2/3 cup brown sugar
- 1/4 cup molasses
- 1 tsp ginger
- 1 1/2 tsp cinnamon
- 1/2 tsp nutmeg
- 1/2 tsp all-spice
- 1 tsp vanilla

Sauce:

- 1 1/2 cup sugar
- 1 1/2 sticks butter, softened
- 14-oz sweetened condensed milk
- 2 tsp vanilla

What to do:

1. Preheat your oven to 350 degrees F and spray a 2 quart baking dish with nonstick spray.
2. Place cubed bread on a baking sheet and bake for about 10 minutes, stirring halfway through.

3. Remove from the oven and place the bread cubes in a large bowl.
4. In another bowl, whisk together the milk, eggs, sugar, molasses, ginger, cinnamon, nutmeg, all spice, and vanilla until combined.
5. Pour the milk and egg mixture over the bread and stir well. Let sit for 10-15 minutes to make sure the bread gets really soaked.
6. Spoon the bread mixture into the 2 quart baking dish and bake for 50-60 minutes or until the center is set.
7. Remove from the oven and let cool slightly.
8. For the sauce, add sugar and butter to a saucepan over medium heat and stir to mix. Cook until melted and creamy. Stir in the condensed milk and vanilla.
9. Pour over bread pudding and serve.

Pumpkin Crisp

Servings: 8

What you need:

- · 1 15-oz can pumpkin
- · 3/4 cup evaporated milk
- · 1 cup sugar
- · 1 tsp vanilla
- · 1/2 tsp cinnamon
- · 1/4 tsp nutmeg
- · 1 yellow cake mix
- · 1 cup chopped pecans
- · 1/2 cup butter, melted

What to do:

1. Stir together the first six ingredients and pour into lightly greased pan.
2. Sprinkle dry cake mix evenly over pumpkin mixture.
3. Top with pecans and drizzle with the melted butter.
4. Bake 1 hour at 350 degrees, until golden brown.
5. Best served warm with cool whip.

Raspberry Cheesecake Cups

Servings: 10

What you need:

· 8 oz cream cheese, at room temperature
· 1 3.4-oz package of vanilla instant pudding mix
· 1 1/2 cups cold milk
· 1 1/2 cups fresh raspberries

What to do:

1. Beat the cream cheese in a medium bowl with an electric mixer until smooth and creamy.
2. Gradually add in the milk and dry pudding mix and beat until smooth.
3. Place raspberries in 10 dessert glasses.
4. Spoon the cream cheese mixture onto the raspberries in each cup.
5. Refrigerate for 2 hours before serving.

Cranberry Christmas Cake

Servings: 16

What you need:

- 3 eggs
- 2 cups sugar
- 3/4 cup butter, softened
- 1 tsp vanilla
- 2 cups all-purpose flour
- 12 oz cranberries, fresh or thawed

What to do:

1. Preheat your oven to 350 degrees F. Spray a 9x13 inch baking dish with nonstick spray.
2. With an electric mixer, beat the eggs and sugar together until thickened, about 5-6 minutes. It should double in size.
3. Add in the butter and vanilla and mix for 2 minutes.
4. Stir in the flour until just combined.
5. Stir in the cranberries.
6. Spread into the prepared dish and bake for 40-50 minutes or until a toothpick inserted into the center comes out clean.
7. Let cool completely then cut into slices and serve.

Christmas Tree Cream Cheese Danish

Servings: 8

What you need:

· 1 can of refrigerated crescent rolls
· 8 oz cream cheese, softened
· 1 can cherry pie filling
· 1/3 cup sugar
· 1 tsp vanilla
· 1/3 cup powdered sugar
· 2 tsp milk

What to do:

1. Preheat your oven to 350 degrees F.
2. Combine the powdered sugar and milk in a small bowl and set aside. This is the glaze.
3. Open the package of crescent rolls but do not unroll or separate them. Use a serrated knife to slice them into 12 equal rounds.
4. Arrange the 12 rounds into the shape of a Christmas tree.
5. Press your thumb down into the center of each round to form an indention.
6. In a mixing bowl with an electric mixer, whip the cream cheese until smooth. Mix in the sugar and vanilla.
7. Place a large spoonful of cream cheese mixture into the indention on each round. Then place a spoonful of cherry pie filling onto each spoonful of cream cheese.

8. Bake for 18-20 minutes.
9. Let cool a bit then drizzle with glaze.

Chocolate Chip Cookie Pie

Servings: 8

What you need:

- 1/2 cup butter, melted
- 1 cup sugar
- 2 eggs
- 1 tsp vanilla
- 1/2 tsp salt
- 1/2 cup flour
- 1 cup chopped pecans
- 1 cup chocolate chips
- 1 frozen pie crust

What to do:

1. Preheat oven to 325 degrees F.
2. Mix the butter and sugar together with an electric mixer until combined.
3. Add in the eggs and vanilla and mix well.
4. Add the salt and flour and mix well.
5. Fold in the pecans and chocolate chips.
6. Pour the mixture into the pie crust and bake for 1 hour.
7. Let cool before slicing.

Gingerbread Spice Cake

Servings: 12

What you need:

· 2 cups all-purpose flour
· 1 tsp baking soda
· 1 1/2 tsp ground ginger
· 2 tsp ground cinnamon
· 1/4 tsp ground cloves
· 1/4 tsp salt
· 3/4 cup molasses
· 3/4 cup hot water
· 1/2 cup butter, at room temperature
· 1/3 cup packed brown sugar
· 1 egg, at room temperature
· 1 tsp vanilla extract

Frosting:

· 8 oz cream cheese, at room temperature
· 2 tbsp butter, at room temperature
· 1 1/2 cups powdered sugar
· 2 tbsp milk
· 1 tsp vanilla extract

What to do:

1. Preheat your oven to 350 degrees F and grease a 9-inch springform pan.
2. In a medium bowl, whisk together the flour, baking soda, ginger, cinnamon, cloves, and salt.
3. In another bowl, whisk together the molasses and hot water.
4. In a large bowl, beat the butter with an electric mixer until smooth and creamy. Add in the brown sugar and beat for one minute, scraping down the sides as needed.
5. Beat in the eggs and vanilla until combined.
6. On low speed, gradually mix the flour mixture and molasses mixture into the butter/sugar mixture.
7. Pour the batter into the prepared pan and bake for 30-40 minutes or until a toothpick inserted comes out clean.
8. Remove from the oven and let the cake cool completely in the pan.
9. To make the frosting, in a large bowl, beat the cream cheese and butter together with an electric mixer. Add in the powdered sugar, milk, and vanilla extract and beat until creamy. Spread on top and on the sides of the cake.

Christmas Trifle

Servings: 10

What you need:

· 1 box devil's food cake, prepared according to package directions
· 1 box instant chocolate pudding, prepared according to package directions
· 16 oz Cool Whip
· 1 21-oz can of cherry filling

What to do:

1. Crumble the cake into small pieces.
2. Layer cake pieces, pudding, cherry filling, and whipped cream. Continue until all ingredients have been used.
3. Refrigerate for at least 2 hours before serving.

Banana Pudding

Servings: 18

What you need:

- 2 boxes Nilla Wafers
- 8 bananas, sliced
- 2 cups whole milk
- 1 5-oz box French vanilla pudding mix
- 8-oz cream cheese
- 14-oz sweetened condensed milk
- 12-oz Cool Whip, thawed

What to do:

1. Line the bottom of a 13x9 inch dish with 1 bag of Nilla Wafers.
2. Layer sliced bananas on top of the wafers.
3. In a large bowl, combine the milk and pudding mix and whisk together well. Cover and refrigerate.
4. In a separate bowl, with an electric mixer, mix up the cream cheese and sweetened condensed milk until smooth.
5. Fold the Cool Whip into the cream cheese mixture.
6. Stir the pudding mixture into the cream cheese/Cool Whip mixture. Mix well.
7. Pour the mixture over the bananas and cookies in the dish.
8. Cover with the rest of the Nilla Wafers.
9. Refrigerate for 2 hours or until ready to serve.

White Chocolate Cheeseball

Servings: 10

What you need:

- 8-oz cream cheese at room temperature
- 2 tbsp brown sugar
- 1/4 cup powdered sugar
- 1 cup white chocolate chips, melted
- 1 1/2 cups chopped walnuts
- Graham crackers, for dipping

What to do:

1. Line a plate with a long piece of plastic wrap. Set aside.
2. With an electric mixer, mix the cream cheese, brown sugar, and powdered sugar until smooth and creamy.
3. Add the melted white chocolate chips and 1/4 cup of chopped walnuts and mix until combined well.
4. Use a rubber spatula to scrape the mixture out onto the long piece of plastic wrap and work the mixture into a ball using the plastic wrap. Wrap the ball in the plastic wrap.
5. Put the ball into the freezer for two hours. It should not freeze through.
6. Place the rest of the chopped walnuts onto a plate.
7. Unwrap the cheeseball and roll it in the chopped walnuts.
8. Place the cheeseball on a serving plate and serve with graham crackers.

Drinks

Holiday Sangria

Servings: 10

What you need:

- 2 bottles Pinot Grigio
- 1 cup sparkling apple cider
- 1/4 cup sugar
- 1/4 cup cranberries, cut in half
- 3/4 cup cranberries, whole
- 1 apple, cored and chopped

What to do:

1. Combine all of the ingredients in a pitcher and stir until the sugar dissolves. Refrigerate for at least 2 hours before serving.

Red Velvet Hot Chocolate

Servings: 4

What you need:

· 4 cups whole milk
· 1/4 cup sugar
· 10 oz chocolate chips
· 2 tsp red food coloring
· 1 tsp vanilla extract
· 1/4 cup heavy cream
· 4 oz cream cheese, at room temperature
· 1/2 cup sugar
· 1/2 tsp salt
· 1/2 tsp vanilla extract

What to do:

1. Bring the milk and 1/4 cup sugar to a simmer in a medium saucepan over medium heat. Stir to dissolve the sugar.
2. Remove from heat and stir in the chocolate chips and stir until melted.
3. Stir in the food coloring and vanilla.
4. Pour into serving cups.
5. To make cream cheese topping, whip the whipping cream with an electric mixer until soft peaks form, 5-10 minutes. Set aside.
6. Place the cream cheese, sugar, salt, and vanilla in a separate bowl and mix with electric mixer until combined and creamy.

7. Fold the whipped cream into the cream cheese mixture by hand. Top the hot chocolate with this topping!

Nutella Hot Chocolate

Servings: 4

What you need:

· 4 cups whole milk
· 3 tbsp Nutella
· 2 tbsp unsweetened cocoa powder
· 2 tbsp raw sugar
· Marshmallows, for topping

What to do:

1. Heat the milk in a medium saucepan over medium high heat until simmering.
2. Whisk in the Nutella, cocoa powder, and sugar and mix until dissolved and smooth.
3. Pour into 4 mugs.
4. Top with marshmallows and serve.

Salted Caramel Eggnog

Servings: 6

What you need:

- 3 cups whole milk
- 1 cup heavy whipping cream
- 4 cinnamon sticks
- 1 tbsp pure vanilla extract
- 1 tsp grated nutmeg
- 5 eggs
- 2/3 cup sugar
- 1/2 cup caramel syrup
- 1 tbsp sea salt
- 3/4 cup dark rum

What to do:

1. In a large saucepan over medium heat, combine the milk, cream, cinnamon, vanilla, and nutmeg. Bring to a strong simmer. Remove from heat and let sit for 10 minutes.
2. In a large mixing bowl, beat the eggs and sugar on medium high with an electric mixer until fully combined.
3. Pour the egg mixture into the milk and whisk to combine.
4. Add the caramel, sea salt, and rum. Continue whisking.
5. Pour into cups and serve.

  **Consume raw eggs at your own risk.

Slow Cooker Gingerbread Latte

Servings: 6-8

What you need:

- 8 cups whole milk
- 1/4 cup maple syrup
- 2 tbsp brown sugar
- 3 tsp ground ginger
- 1 tsp vanilla
- 2 cinnamon sticks
- A pinch of cloves
- 1/2 tsp nutmeg
- 3 1/2 cups strongly brewed coffee or espresso
- Whipped cream and gingerbread man cookies, for garnish

What to do:

1. Add all the ingredients except for the garnishes to your slow cooker and stir.
2. Cook on low for 3 hours, make sure it doesn't boil.
3. Turn the slow cooker to the lowest setting (mine is "keep warm") and cook for another 2 hours.
4. Stir right before serving.
5. Dip into cups and garnish with whipped cream and cookies.

Mint White Hot Chocolate

Servings: 4

What you need:

· 2 cups whole milk
· 2 cups half and half
· 12 oz white chocolate chips
· 1 tsp peppermint extract
· 1/2 tsp vanilla extract
· Green food coloring, optional

What to do:

1. In a large saucepan, add the milk and half and half. Heat over medium until it reaches a light simmer.
2. Stir in the white chocolate chips and stir until melted.
3. Stir in the peppermint and vanilla and food coloring if you're using it.
4. Scoop into cups and serve.

White Christmas Punch

Servings: 12-16

What you need:

- · 1/2 cup sugar
- · 1/4 cup hot water
- · 3 oz evaporated milk
- · 1 tsp almond extract
- · 1/2 gallon vanilla ice-cream
- · 2 liters of 7-UP
- · Whipped cream and Christmas sprinkles, for garnish

What to do:

1. In a glass bowl, stir together the sugar and hot water until the sugar is dissolved.
2. Cool the sugar water and stir in the evaporated milk and almond extract.
3. Pour the mixture into a large punch bowl and add the vanilla ice cream.
4. Use a couple of big spoons or a potato masher to break the ice cream up a bit.
5. Slowly pour in the 7 up.
6. Serve in glasses topped with whipped cream and Christmas sprinkles.

Peppermint Hot Chocolate

Servings: 4

What you need:

- 2/3 cup heavy whipping cream
- 8 peppermints, crushed
- 4 cups milk
- 8 oz white chocolate, chopped
- 1/2 tsp peppermint extract
- Crushed peppermints, for garnish

What to do:

1. In a medium bowl with a mixer, beat the heavy whipping cream and crushed peppermints until stiff peaks form. Cover and refrigerate.
2. In a large saucepan, heat the milk over medium heat.
3. Add the white chocolate to the milk and whisk until it is melted completely.
4. Stir in the peppermint extract.
5. Ladle the hot chocolate into mugs and top with the whipped cream mixture from the refrigerator.
6. Top the whipped cream with crushed peppermints and serve.

Free Gift

Breakfast, Lunch, Dinner, Soups, Salads, Desserts and More!

Simply visit: www.HanniepScott.com/freegift

Notes

Notes

Made in the
USA
Monee, IL